RENEWING THE MIND:
The Key To Transformation

by
Casey Treat

Harrison House
Tulsa, Oklahoma

Cover by Tim Hodgson
Kirkland, Washington

8th Printing
Over 62,000 in Print

Renewing The Mind: The Key To Transformation
ISBN 0-931697-23-9
Copyright © 1992 by Casey D. Treat
P.O. Box 98800
Seattle, Washington 98198

Published by Harrison House, Inc.
P.O. Box 35035
Tulsa, Oklahoma 74153

CONTENTS

1. The Greatest Day Of My Life   7

2. Being Born Of The Spirit   11

3. Renewing The Mind:
   What It Is And What It Does   17

4. Change Is The Way Of Life   25

5. Defining The Soul   33

6. The Power Of The Truth   41

7. The Mind: Control Center Of Your Life   49

8. Control Your Mind And Control Your Destiny   57

9. The Great Exchange   65

10. Five Areas Where Our Minds
    Must Be Renewed   71

11. Change: Learn To Love It   81

12. No Quick Fixes   87

13. The Master Key   93

Dedication

This book is dedicated to Julius Young, who introduced me to Jesus. Through spending hours of discussion on renewing the mind, Julius became a personal friend and leader whom I loved. Julius died in 1989. He was the Founder of the Washington Drug Rehabilitation Center and a spiritual father to many people.

1
The Greatest Day Of My Life

It was September of '74, and I found myself sitting in the hallway of the Washington Drug Rehabilitation Center. I was in shock having just been given a choice by the county judge either to go to prison for a minimum of a year, or enter rehabilitation for at least two years. As I sat there, I thought, "I'm really not that bad. I've just had a few unlucky breaks that keep landing me in jail. It isn't my fault. It's the police or the school administration or society or something, but not me. Just ask my mom, she'll tell you; it's the crowd I hang with."

Reality began to sink in as I went through a very difficult interview and was finally accepted into the program. While I was scared, mad, and embarrassed that I needed to be "put away" to get my head together, I was also excited and desired a new life. By nineteen, I had ruined my health both physically and mentally, filled several file folders of various reports at the county jail, and alienated my family and friends. Though I denied it on the inside, I really wanted to change, but how could I?

Somehow I had bought into the concept that you are what you are, and there's nothing you can do about it. I soon learned that I could change and make my life whatever I wanted it to be. It would not be an instantaneous experience, but it would be a miraculous one. As my life began to be reshaped, rebuilt, and renewed, I found I had a destiny in God, and the opportunity to live a rewarding lifestyle with a purpose. I also found out that most people are like I was in that they don't like some part of their lives, but feel unable to do anything about it.

The purpose for this revised edition of *Renewing The*

Mind, is to assist you in becoming all that you were predestined and purposed to be. If you will invest the time and energy to absorb the following pages, you will have the Biblical truths you need to change, grow, and become all you can be. Whatever your present place in life, you have the potential to move forward, and experience more of God's will and plan. You may be starting with an element of success in life; others are starting at the foundational level. Wherever you are, let's go together toward God's best and your destiny.

RENEWING THE MIND KEY #1

YOU CAN CHANGE TO MAKE
YOUR LIFE WHAT YOU WANT
IT TO BE.

Renewing the mind is a journey I've been on for the past eighteen years. I've gone from being an average American teenager who didn't like himself, or anything about life, to a husband, father, and pastor who is enjoying the blessing of the Lord in every way. The truths you will learn in the following pages are neither my ideas or thoughts nor are they the hype of another self-help message; they are the principles from the Word of God.

I learned long ago, that if you have a map of the wrong city, no matter how good your attitude, how positive your confession, or how excited your spirit, you will stay lost, and not get to your desired destination. There are dozens of ''positive'' teachers and writers but they don't give you the right principles to be positive. Once you have the right map, you can use your positive attitude, positive confession, and positive spirit to move you toward the goals of your life. The Bible provides us with such direction.

The Bible is the map, or principles, that will get us where we want to go, both eternally as well as for day-to-day living. All the philosophies of the world have proven to be inadequate and bring failure. Our broken marriages, children, economy, and nation are evidence of that. The Word of God may not be popular, but it alone gives the principles that guide us to happy families, healthy lives, and fulfilled destinies. If we will renew our way of thinking to principles in the Bible, we will find the success in life we so desperately desire.

I believe every Christian, and most non-Christians, desire to change their lives and find a higher way, but they don't know how, and feel unable. The fact is you can change and be all God planned for you to be. He has predestined you for greatness spiritually, mentally, physically, and financially. Your marriage, family, career, and self-esteem can and should be exciting and fulfilling. Let's start our journey on God's map for renewing of the mind, and the fulfilling of your destiny.

2
Being Born Of The Spirit

One of the first lessons I learned as I began to build a new life was that my spirit was separated from God's Spirit. To really change my life, I needed more than a new job, girlfriend, or counselor. I needed a relationship with the One who created me and destined me for a fulfilled life. I could not have a relationship with God, an eternal destiny with Him, or His power in my life on earth until I was changed spiritually. This is more than going to church, saying a prayer (which I had done many times in jail), or becoming religious. In fact, becoming religious was one of the things I certainly did not want to do, and still don't.

My first step was to be born again. The way Jesus said it in the Bible is not the way some new age guru or motivational preacher would say it. To be born again, is to be spiritually recreated. Paul said in **2 Corinthians 5:17: Therefore, if anyone is in Christ, he is a new creation; old things have passed away; behold, all things have become new.** I was already physically born, but I needed to be spiritually born. Jesus said in **John 3:3,6: ...most assuredly, I say to you, unless one is born again, he cannot see the kingdom of God. That which is born of the flesh is flesh, and that which is born of the Spirit is spirit.**

You are a spirit being who lives in a physical body. Your body is alive, but until the "second" birth, "new" birth or until you're "born again," your spirit is dead or separated from God. It exists, but it cannot contact the Father, and you have no spiritual relationship with Him. You may believe in God, know about God, and have religious behavior; but Jesus said you must be born again or you will never see the Kingdom of God. In fact, **James 2:19** tells us:

11

You believe that there is one God. You do well. Even the demons believe — and tremble! The devil trembles in God's presence, but he certainly has no eternal relationship with Him.

When we are born again, our spirit is changed, and we become joined to the Holy Spirit. **Second Corinthians 3:17: Now the Lord is the Spirit; and where the Spirit of the Lord is, there is liberty. Romans 10:9,10: . . . if you confess with your mouth the Lord Jesus and believe in your heart that God has raised Him from the dead, you will be saved** (new birth). **For with the heart one believes to righteousness, and with the mouth confession is made to salvation.**

This new beginning is a spiritual change, not a physical, or mental change. When you become a "new creation," it's obvious your body doesn't change. I still had red hair, was still 6'3", and needed to exercise more. You may be bald, overweight, skinny, muscular, or weak; none of these things change with the new birth. The same is true for the mind. I had the same fears, bad attitudes, questions, desires, and thoughts, after I was born again as I did before. This is not a mental process, it is a spiritual one.

```
┌─    RENEWING THE MIND KEY #2    ─┐
│                                   │
│    THE NEW BIRTH CHANGES MY       │
│    SPIRIT, BUT NOT MY MIND OR     │
│       PHYSICAL BODY.              │
│                                   │
└───────────────────────────────────┘
```

Being born again is the beginning, but sad to say, for most Christians, it's also the end when it comes to growing with God. They never learn the next step (which takes the rest of our lives here on earth), and go on to Christian growth and spiritual maturity. While our spirit is recreated, or born again, instantly when we make Jesus the Lord of our life, our mind, which is part of the soul, must be changed through an on-going process. It is not an instantaneous change, and it takes discipline, determination, and desire to bring it to pass. It's called *renewing the mind*. Though it is the key to all Christian growth, most Christians do little of it because of a lack of knowledge or a lack of discipline.

Let me share a natural, physical example of this spiritual truth. I delivered our three children in our home. Though my part was much easier than my wife Wendy's (especially since Caleb was 10 lbs. 10 ozs., Tasha was 10 lbs., and Micah was 6 weeks early at 7 lbs.), I can still testify that birthing those little critters was much easier than raising them. The birth was a matter of moments, but raising them is an on-going process of teaching, training, and loving, for many years.

So it is in the Christian life. To be born again takes a commitment to Jesus as Lord, and there is an instant change in your spirit. To grow spiritually is an on-going process of renewing your mind to the Word of God, reprogramming your thoughts with the thoughts of God, exchanging the way you think in the natural mind to the way God says we should think.

Paul said in **1 Thessalonians 5:23: Now may the God of peace Himself sanctify you completely; and may your whole spirit, soul, and body be preserved blameless at the coming of our Lord Jesus Christ.** The Christian walk is more than a spiritual change. It includes the soul and body. The soul is your mind, emotions, and will (Chapter 5 gives a complete definition of the soul). If we are to walk with God and fulfill our destinies as Christians, then we must deal with the whole person — spirit, soul, and body.

Paul says we are to be sanctified "completely" or "wholly." We must go beyond the new birth, though we cannot add to this complete work of salvation in a spiritual sense, we can change our soul, and to some degree, our body. Salvation of the spirit man is an eternal work that cannot be earned, improved or added to, but the salvation of the soul is another subject.

Ephesians 2:8,9 says: **For by grace you have been saved through faith, and that not of yourselves; it is the gift of God, not of works, lest anyone should boast.** I can't work for my spiritual salvation; Jesus provided it for me. Those religions that have their people selling magazines, doing missions work or trying to earn some eternal blessing through prayers, candles, money, or anything else, do not understand the work that Jesus did for all mankind. There is nothing I can do to deserve or improve the new birth. I can never be saved spiritually by works.

However, I do work for the salvation of my soul. This was not a finished work at the cross of Calvary. Paul says in **I Corinthians 1:18: For the message of the cross is foolishness to those who are perishing, but to us who are being saved it is the power of God.** And, in **Philippians 2:12,** Paul writes: ...**work out your own salvation with fear and trembling.** While Paul said we are not saved by works, James said in **James 1:21, Therefore lay aside all filthiness and overflow of wickedness, and receive with meekness the implanted word, which is able to SAVE YOUR SOULS.** He's writing to Christians who are already spiritually saved, but they need to work out the soulish aspect of their salvation by receiving the Word of God in their lives and changing their behavior to line up with it.

STEPS TO PERSONAL TRANSFORMATION

1. When did I make Jesus the Lord of my life and experience the new birth?

2. If you are not born again, pray this prayer:
   "Heavenly Father, I confess Jesus is Lord of my life. I believe Jesus was raised from the dead. I turn away from the sin and negativity of my life and turn to Jesus to lead and guide my life. Thank You, Lord Jesus, for coming into my heart and giving me a new spirit. I will learn from You and follow You from this day forward."

3. How have I renewed my mind since I was born again?

4. What three areas of my life need the most renewal at this time?

5. Do I really want growth and change in my life?

3
Renewing The Mind:
What It Is And What It Does

The most powerful verse of scripture God used in my first Christian years, and still does, is **Romans 12:2: And do not be conformed to this world, but be TRANS-FORMED BY THE RENEWING OF YOUR MIND, that you may prove what is that good and acceptable and perfect will of God.** Through this verse, I learned that even though I was a Christian, I was still conformed to the world and all of its negativity, failure, and problems until my mind was renewed. I was on my way to heaven, because I had been born again; but I could live like hell until I got there.

So many Christians struggle through life with negative attitudes, sin, failures, divorce, depression, and wonder why it's all happening to them. Some have built a doctrine to explain their lifestyle of defeat, and blame the sovereignty of God, or some such thing, for all their troubles. The fact is, they are still conformed to the world, because their mind has not been renewed, so they cannot prove the good, acceptable, and perfect will of God in their life. The Lord said through **James** in chapter **1:13-15, Let no one say when he is tempted, "I am tempted by God"; for God cannot be tempted by evil, nor does He Himself tempt anyone. But each one is tempted when he is drawn away by his own desires and enticed. Then, when desire has conceived, it gives birth to sin; and sin, when it is full-grown, brings forth death.** When our mind is renewed to the Word of God, we will overcome negative desires, and live God's perfect will.

RENEWING THE MIND KEY #3

YOU CAN BE ON YOUR WAY TO HEAVEN, BUT LIVE IN HELL ON EARTH.

If a person is still depressed, afraid of life, and circumstances, treating their spouse badly, struggling in poverty, having sex with someone they are not married to, caught up in pornography, mad at the world or any such things, though they may be born again, they are still conformed to the world. Some would believe that if you ever sin in these ways, you could not be born again. But John says in I John, chapter 1, that we will sin, but we can receive forgiveness if we confess our sin to Jesus. If we say we never sin we are lying.

The point is that Christians will mess up, but we can be forgiven. Through renewing the mind, we overcome those failures, and we don't have to live in them. We do not have to be conformed, fashioned, molded, or controlled by the ways of the world; we can walk with God, and prove, display, and be an example of His will.

To be TRANSFORMED is to go through a complete change in form or kind. The Greek word used in this verse is "metamorpho." It means to go through a complete change in form such as the caterpillar does when it comes out of its cocoon, as a butterfly. It doesn't just add some wings to its furry, long body. It completely changes into a different kind of being that can do totally different things and live a totally different life. The Christian will begin to see the fullness of his salvation, live a completely different life than before, and accomplish great things when he is transformed by the renewing of the mind.

RENEWING THE MIND KEY #4

RENEWING THE MIND IS
MORE THAN LEARNING;
IT IS CHANGING.

So many people come to church to learn something new, and add to their intellectual insights. They feel good if the sermon was stimulating, intriguing, or exciting; but they never consider changing the way they think or live. They are so far, far away from changing that they really don't make a decision not to change; they don't even think about it.

For so long, the Bible and church have been religious traditions that were not a part of the real world and our daily lifestyles. We must make some major adjustments in our thinking to just get started in the renewing the mind process.

Many Christians have been taught that if they just read their Bible, pray, and go to church regularly, they will become stronger Christians. It's too bad we never examined the fruit of that thinking, because the fact is, there are a multitude of people who have done those things all their lives and are not happy, prosperous, successful people.

Romans 12:2 clearly shows us there is more to Christian growth than that. It's possible to read the Bible, pray and go to church and never renew your mind. The person who sins all week but is a faithful church attender proves that. The pastor who preaches great sermons, and then commits adultery proves that. Renewing the mind is so much more than going through religious motions. It is a conscious effort and labor to:

1. Become aware of how we really think and believe,
2. Become aware of how God wants us to think,
3. Focus our thoughts on God's thoughts,
4. Practice the thoughts of God until they are our own, and
5. Live the thoughts of God with our actions in everyday life.

This process then must be repeated time and time again as we come into situations where attitudes and thoughts arise that are contrary to the Word of God. It is not an overnight change. It cannot be received by the laying on of hands, but rather a lifestyle that we will follow until we meet the Lord in the air **(1 John 3:2: . . . when He is revealed, we shall be like Him. . .).**

```
┌─      RENEWING THE MIND KEY #5      ─┐

        RENEWING THE MIND
           IS A LIFESTYLE,
        NOT AN EXPERIENCE.

└──────────────────────────────────────┘
```

If we ever want to see the good, acceptable, and perfect will of God in our lives, we must get on with the renewing of our minds. Paul says this is the only way the necessary transformation can take place. Many Christians are not seeing all of God's promises being fulfilled in their lives. Many who say they are Christians, have no lifestyle to back it up. The way these things will be changed is through the transformation of our lives, and that happens by the renewing of our minds.

Most of us have areas in our lives that are going along pretty well. We have developed right thinking in those areas, and it seems as though we don't have as much trouble there as in some other aspect of life. Some people do well with money, but struggle with relationships; others do well with family but struggle with their health. There are those who seem to be doing well in every aspect of life, but carry secrets of fornication, pornography, and the like.

We must be renewing our mind in all areas of Christian life, and realize that being successful in one aspect does not mean we are successful. If I am a great minister but lose my children to the world, then I am not successful. I may be strong and have a renewed mind in certain areas, but I must press on to deal with every part of the thought life.

Second Corinthians 10:4,5 says: For the weapons of our warfare are not carnal but mighty in God for pulling down strongholds, casting down arguments and every high thing that exalts itself against the knowledge of God, *bringing every thought into captivity to the obedience of Christ.* Strongholds are those thoughts and attitudes, that have such a grip on your mind, that even though you don't want to think that way, you do anyway. You feel like your mind is controlling you, and you can't stop thinking in a certain way.

There are many people who feel terrible about the things that go on in their mind, and the things those thoughts cause them to do. We've all seen or heard people that don't want to do the things they do, but feel like they can't stop. The fact is, you can stop that thought process, but it is a stronghold that must be overcome by capturing those thoughts and making them obey the Word of God.

When a person is consumed with any negative or worldly way of thinking, over a period of time, it becomes a stronghold. The man who thinks about violence, cursing, and proving his manliness, will soon have a bad temper, and end up fighting with anyone who opposes him or steps on his pride. The one who watches or reads pornography regularly will soon be consumed with sexual fantasies and desires that will control his thought life, and cause him to seek for ungodly, and unnatural fulfillment (though he never will be fulfilled because he is trapped in a way of thinking that will destroy him). The woman who watches soap operas will soon be unsatisfied with her husband, or life, and begin to fantasize about other men, or situations which follow the example of the programs that fill her mind.

When a marriage of ten, twenty, or thirty years ends in divorce, there have been years of thoughts about other people and other situations that finally led to the divorce. Many of these thoughts come from the examples and messages that they get from television shows and other media input.

Jesus said we must be careful of what we hear, because we soon will be controlled by it, whether it is good or bad. **Mark 4:24: ...Take heed what you hear. With the same measure you use, it will be measured to you; and to you who hear, more will be given. Proverbs 23:7** says: **For as he thinks in his heart, so is he.** This is why we must guard our minds, and not allow negative strongholds to take control over us. If these things are already there, then we must go to work, capture every thought, and drive them out by the thoughts of God.

Strongholds of fear, anger, poverty, low self-esteem, pride, and selfishness, are controlling many Christians. Though they have prayed about them and tried to get deliverance, these things will not change until they are transformed by the renewing of their minds. This is not to say that some bondages and negative behaviors in Christians are not caused by demon oppression, and in these cases, the demon must be cast off. But even in cases of demon activity, if there is not a renewal of the mind, the enemy will come back; and Jesus said the end of that person will be worse than the beginning (Matthew 12:43-45).

Renewing the mind is an exciting journey of change and discovery, that enables us to see God's will come to pass in our lives. There is no greater joy or fulfillment than to know that we are fulfilling the perfect will of God. And there is no other way (according to the Bible) to prove the will of God in our lives than by the renewing of the mind.

STEPS TO PERSONAL TRANSFORMATION

1. What does the Bible mean when it says "be not conformed to the world"?

2. In what three areas am I still "conformed to the world"?

3. What is Biblical TRANSFORMATION?

4. Why is renewing the mind more than learning?

5. What things have I learned from the Lord but have not yet renewed or changed?

4

Change Is The Way Of Life

...Reproofs of instruction are the way of life, Proverbs
6:23. Reproofs, corrections, instruction, or confrontation
from the Word of God are designed to bring change to our
lives. In this verse, Solomon, the author of Proverbs, tells
us that change is the way of life. If we want to walk with
God, have His perfect will, and experience the fullness of
His plan for our lives, we must continually change. This
is the transformation that Paul is talking about in Romans
12:2. It's a lifestyle of being corrected and instructed, so that
we will move forward in Christian growth.

Throughout the book of Proverbs, the words *reproof,
reprove, rebuke, correct, instruct,* and *teach* show us that to
have the wisdom, and ways of God, we must be willing
to change. As stated in chapter 1, renewing the mind is more
than learning, and change is more than just gaining new
insight or information. The process of change has as much
to do with "taking off" as it does "putting on." It is as much
subtracting, as it is adding.

In **Ephesians 4:22-24** we read: **That you put off,
concerning your former conduct, the old man which grows
corrupt according to the deceitful lusts, and be renewed
in the spirit of your mind, and that you put on the new
man which was created according to God, in righteousness
and true holiness.**

RENEWING THE MIND KEY #6

RENEWING THE MIND IS
BOTH TAKING OFF OLD
THOUGHTS, AND PUTTING
ON THE THOUGHTS OF GOD.

God uses the "taking off" and "putting on" principle throughout the New Testament. In the process of renewing the mind, we must realize that there are as many thoughts and attitudes that must be taken off as there are that must be put on. It is possible to learn many good things, but also possible to never take off the things that keep you from success.

The college graduate has more than enough knowledge to succeed in his area of study; but if he has a negative mind-set, he will stay poor and not see success. The one who knows all about nutrition and exercise will still be overweight and out of shape unless he has removed the negative thoughts and habits that create an unhealthy lifestyle.

It is obvious that just hearing or learning the truth is not all there is to being free. Jesus said it is as we "abide" or live in His Word that we will "know" the truth, and then we will be free, John 8:31,32. The word "know" in this verse means to understand in an experiential way. This means there is something that has been removed, taken out, or taken off, and then replaced by the truth. This is when the truth will really set you free.

So many Christians can quote scriptures about finance, health, marriage, or family, but they are not free in these areas. Learning the verse doesn't mean you have changed. Just learning a passage of scripture does not mean you will be free. The thoughts that are not in line with the thoughts of God must be replaced or rejected by truth. The new man cannot be put on without the old man being taken off.

> ## RENEWING THE MIND KEY #7
>
> TAKING OFF THE OLD MAN
> IS AS IMPORTANT AS
> PUTTING ON THE NEW.

I've had the joy of being a father for the past seven years. At the writing of this edition, Caleb is our first-born, Tasha is five, and Micah is two. As I have said earlier, Wendy and I delivered all three in our home (she did all the hard work, I just did the catching). It didn't take me long to learn that these little critters need plenty of attention, especially on one end of the anatomy. They were calling for a diaper change either by their smell or their whines every couple of hours. If I would have sprinkled a little powder on that old diaper, and put a new one over the top of it, their need would not have been met. They were not changed, until the old one was taken off, and the new one was put on. If we had just covered up the old, I wonder how long it would have taken for the aroma of the dirty diaper to rise through the cover of the clean one.

There are many Christians who want to put on the clean, but don't want to deal with the dirty. They're putting new thoughts in, but it's not long before the old thoughts start coming through, and their life is back in the same old problems. They're like the park built on the garbage dump. The grass was pretty, and the flowers smelled good, but it wasn't long before the garbage, and gasses began to come through. You cannot build a successful Christian life on negative thinking or a garbage foundation. Change involves removing the old, as well as installing the new.

Remember the old saying, "Don't curse the darkness—light a candle"? This holds true when it comes to renewing the mind. Taking off the old and putting on the new are simultaneous changes. We can't sit down and try to make negative thoughts leave our mind. The whole time we are trying to make them leave, we're thinking on the thoughts we don't want. We drive out the old, as we focus our thoughts on the new. We must not spend our time trying to not think about the old thoughts of fear, anger, sin, but rather to think on the things the scripture commands.

Philippians 4:8: Finally, brethren, whatever things are true, whatever things are noble, whatever things are just, whatever things are pure, whatever things are lovely, whatever things are of good report, if there is any virtue and if there is anything praiseworthy — meditate on these things. *The Amplified Bible* says, **fix your minds on them.** We need to be aware of and resist our old carnal thoughts, but we must give ourselves to meditating, pondering, focusing and fixing our mind on the thoughts of God.

Change is not an easy thing. We are programmed from our childhood that once we're out of school, we stop growing. Except for functional learning, we usually don't make any changes in our lifestyle. In fact, we build facades and images to act like we know everything, and try not to change. We want to give the impression that we've got it all together and don't need to change. Then there are the family traditions, religious traditions, and just fleshly stubbornness that keep us from growing and changing. We must make change a positive thing, not something we avoid.

RENEWING THE MIND KEY #8

CHANGE MUST BE A POSITIVE
PART OF OUR LIVES, NOT
SOMETHING WE AVOID.

The people of Israel did not enter their promised land when they could have because they refused to change. The generation that came out of Egypt had a slavery mind-set and would not change it. They murmured at the leadership of Moses, and argued with the commands of the Lord. Though they had many signs from heaven to follow, like the pillar of cloud by day, and pillar of fire by night, they would not let go of their old mentality. As they stood on the border of their land that flowed with milk and honey, they listened to the evil report of the ten spies and the whole multitude began to cry and murmur about their situation. Joshua and Caleb tried to lead them in faith in obedience to God, but the people refused.

Numbers 13:33 says: . . . **we were like grasshoppers in our own sight, and so we were in their sight.** They had not changed their way of thinking from their slavery mentality in Egypt. Though God was with them, called them His people, and promised to take them into the promised land, they would not accept it. Their grasshopper mentality kept them from the promises of God. God had taken them out of Egypt, but He could not take Egypt out of them. That was their responsibility. They were to receive the Word of the Lord through Moses and reject their old way of thinking. But they did not want to change. Their minds were focused on going back to the old life, not pressing on to the new one. They meditated on lies rather than truth.

God had given them the truth that would set them free, but they still believed the lies that kept them in bondage. Because of their refusal to change, they all died in the wilderness. God used Caleb and Joshua to bring their children into the promised land forty years later. How many Christians hang on to the thoughts, and attitudes of the world, and never renew their mind to the Word of God? They stay in their wilderness of depression, sin, stress, poverty or whatever problem may come along, and they never experience the promised land God has given them. **John 10:10 says: The thief does not come except to steal, and to kill, and to destroy. I have come that they may have life, and that they may have it more abundantly.**

Abundant life has been provided, but you must possess it. It will not fall on you like rain from the sky. If you are not willing to change, renew your mind, and go for it, you may live your whole life without all that God has provided for you.

STEPS TO PERSONAL TRANSFORMATION

1. _____ is the way of life.

2. Do I like change or do what I can to avoid it?

3. What "promised lands" have I missed because of an unrenewed mind?

4. Are there parts of my past life that I hang on to or want to go back to?

5. How can I start moving into more of my "promised land" today?

5

Defining The Soul

The Apostle John was an old man when he wrote one of the last letters to be included in the canon of scripture. He had walked with Jesus since he was a young man. His revelations in the Gospel of John cause us to realize the depth of his relationship and understanding of the Lord. It was after many years of Christian life, that John wrote, **Beloved, I pray that you may prosper in all things and be in health, just as your soul prospers, III John 2.** John realized that the prosperity of our whole life, as well as the health of our bodies, hinged on the condition of our soul. It is what is in us that controls what comes out of us and ultimately all of life's experiences. The old apostle is telling us that, even as our soul prospers, our life will prosper.

So many Christians wonder about God's will when it comes to prosperity and health. It is quite obvious that John would not pray a prayer that was contrary to the will of God. He also wouldn't say he prayed this prayer above every other. If it was not God's will that His people prosper, and live in health, the Holy Spirit would certainly not have recorded this as a part of Holy Scripture.

The key to this passage is the soul. Theologians refer to the soul as the mind, emotions, and will. There is much more that can and will be said to define the soul, but this is a good place to start:

* Your mind — reasoning and thinking processes,
* Your emotions — feelings,
* Your will — deciding and choosing processes.

These things make up the soul, and control, to a great degree, how you experience life. You will prosper and live in health even as your soul prospers, or you will struggle, and be weak, even as your soul is weak.

```
┌─  RENEWING THE MIND KEY #9  ─┐

   YOUR SOUL, MIND, EMOTIONS,
 AND WILL MUST PROSPER, BEFORE
   YOUR LIFE WILL PROSPER.

└──────────────────────────────┘
```

The prophet **Hosea** said in **chapter 4, verse 6: My people are destroyed for lack of knowledge. Because you have rejected knowledge, I also will reject you from being priest for Me.** Lack of knowledge devastates many Christians and holds them in a life of mediocrity. One of the greatest areas of confusion and lack of knowledge is the definition of the *soul* and *spirit*. Some teachers say they are the same thing. Some say they are different, but function together in harmony. While this is not a theological treatise, I do want to give some scriptural definition of the soul, and spirit because it is crucial to living out the Word of God. If we don't know what the Lord is telling us to do, there is no way we can do it; therefore, we are destroyed for lack of knowledge.

First Thessalonians 5:23 says: Now may the God of peace Himself sanctify you completely; and may your whole spirit, soul, and body be preserved blameless at the coming of our Lord Jesus Christ. Paul is praying that we be preserved "completely" or "wholly," every part of our being. Then he lists each part of the human person: the spirit, soul and body. This verse illustrates the uniqueness of the spirit and the soul. Your spirit is sanctified or made pure when you are born again. **First Corinthians 6:17 says: But who is joined to the Lord is one spirit with Him.**

The ongoing sanctification of our lives takes place in the soul, and body, where the new birth has not brought change.

To continue our definition of the soul, let's look at **Hebrews 4:12: For the word of God is living and powerful, and sharper than any two-edged sword, piercing even to the division of soul and spirit, and of joints and marrow, and is a discerner of the thoughts and intents of the heart.** Here we see that the Word is the final authority in all the issues of life. It alone will infallibly discern what is from the Lord, Spirit, and what is from man, soul. Only the Word is the final authority when judging the thoughts and intents of the heart of man. As we dissect this verse a bit more, I think you'll get some insight to the functions of the soul and spirit of man:

Soul--------------------------------Spirit,
Joints---------------------------Marrow,
Thoughts-----------------------Intents
Of The Heart.

The writer of Hebrews, by inspiration of the Holy Spirit, relates *Soul - Joints - Thoughts.* Your soul is a connector for your spirit and body. It brings the spirit realm and the physical realm into relationship so you can live as a spiritual being in relation to God, and function in a natural world. As you hear things in your spirit which is born of the Holy Spirit, it is heard in your soul. Sometimes you "just know"; sometimes you'll say "something told me"; sometimes, you'll feel as if the Holy Spirit had just spoken to you. This is the process of the soul connecting the spirit and body as a joint.

Then we see the soul is related to thoughts. This is the major tool and function of the soul. Your thoughts are directing your decisions, actions, and feelings every day. Your thoughts take place in your soul.

Notice the spirit of man is related to marrow and intents. Marrow is the life-giving force, where blood is created in the bones. The Old Testament tells us, "Life is in the blood." Intents are the deep desires and purposes of our heart. Both of these things describe the spirit man.

Understanding that the soul is not the same as the spirit, you can see why it is possible to be a born again Christian with a saved spirit, but struggle in life because of an unrenewed soul. This is why God tells every believer to be "transformed by the renewing of your mind," Romans 12:2. Though your spirit is saved, your soul is being saved as you renew your mind, emotions and will to the Word of God. To the degree that you do this your life will prosper and you will be in health.

These truths enable us to understand scriptures like **Proverbs 23:7: For as he thinks in his heart, so is he. Matthew 22:37 says: . . . You shall love the Lord your God with all your heart, with all your soul, and with all your mind.** The habitual thoughts of our life control how we live. Jesus commands us to do more than just believe in God, but love Him with our heart; then He gets more specific, our soul, and finally He makes it crystal clear, with our mind. To love the Lord with "all" that is within us, we must remove every thought that is not loving Him.

```
┌─ RENEWING THE MIND KEY #10 ─┐

    THE SOUL AND SPIRIT
    OF MAN MAKE UP THE
    HEART OF MAN.

└─────────────────────────────┘
```

At the end of Hebrews 4:12, did you note the phrase "of the heart"? The spirit and soul make up the heart of man. At different times throughout the scripture, heart is used to describe the whole person or a particular part of the inner man of a person. **Second Corinthians 4:16** says: **...Even though our outward man is perishing, yet the inward man is being renewed day by day.** Paul cannot be talking about the human spirit since it was born again when you made Jesus Lord of your life. He's saying the inward man, which is made up of "spirit and soul," is being renewed as we walk with the Lord, even though our outward man, physical body, is getting older and dying.

Part of Christian growth is getting to a place where we can follow our spirit and not our flesh. The flesh is constantly desiring worldly, carnal, negative things, but the spirit is joined to the Lord and desires godly things. The soul hears, and can follow either the spirit or the flesh. Remember, it is the joint or connector. When your spirit says, "I want to pray for thirty minutes and seek the Lord this morning," but your flesh says, "I want to stay in bed and then watch TV," your soul is the controller; and *you* must decide which one you're going to follow. The weak Christian will follow the flesh; the strong Christian will go with the leading of his spirit. The reason God is so concerned with the sanctification or purifying and renewal of your soul is because without it, you will be constantly controlled by your fleshly desires.

A prosperous soul is one that hears and chooses to follow the spirit man. Then, we are promised that we will prosper, and live in health in every realm of life. This prosperity is not an extravagant lust for money, or material things. It is having your needs met and abundance enough to be a blessing to those around you.

RENEWING THE MIND KEY #11

THE PROSPEROUS SOUL HEARS,
AND AGREES WITH THE SPIRIT.

Those who question their salvation experience, and wonder if they are really saved are usually people who have a weak soul, and so they are controlled by their flesh. They struggle to live for the Lord, but feel as if they cannot obey the Spirit, and consequently feel unsaved. As the soul is strengthened through the Word of God, and it begins to prosper, their whole life begins to prosper, and they sense the Holy Spirit working in their spirit. He was there all the time, but they could not follow Him because of their soul.

Let's look at eight things that constitute a poor soul and how these can be turned into elements of a prosperous soul:

1. Having lack of knowledge of the Bible (Hosea 4:6),

2. Being controlled by the desires of the flesh — cannot control weight, spending, sexual lusts (Romans 8:5),

3. Being weak, indecisive, or double-minded (James 1:8),

4. Fantasizing on negativity, and not being able to control your thoughts (II Corinthians 10:4,5),

5. Refusing to change, defending past behavior, and excusing yourself (Proverbs 9:7-9),

6. Spending all your life on natural, earthly, material things (Colossians 3:1,2),

7. Allowing emotions to control attitudes and behaviors (Ephesians 4:22-24),

8. Allowing fear, anger, bitterness, gossip or negative thinking to consume you (Philippians 4:8).

RENEWING THE MIND KEY #12

THROUGH THE WORD OF GOD
AND SINCERE EFFORT,
THE POOR SOUL CAN
BE MADE PROSPEROUS.

Now, here are eight elements of a *prosperous* soul:

1. Being hungry to learn and change (Matthew 5:6),

2. Having a mind that meditates God's Word and follows its precepts (Psalm 1:1-3),

3. Having a disciplined mind and will that agree with the spirit (Romans 8:6),

4. Focusing on godly thoughts and attitudes (Matthew 6:33),

5. Confessing your faults openly and seeking change (James 5:16),

6. Having a mind that is set on things that heaven and God are involved with (Colossians 3:1-10),

7. Having control over feelings and emotions (II Corinthians 5:17),

8. Having a pure, positive, happy attitude towards life (Philippians 4:8).

STEPS TO PERSONAL TRANSFORMATION

1. I must prosper in my _____ before I will prosper in other realms of life.

2. My soul is made of my _____, _____ and _____.

3. My heart is made of my _____ and _____.

4. How has my soul agreed with the flesh and brought defeat to a part of my life?

5. Of the eight things listed, what are the three main things that cause my soul to be poor?

6

The Power Of The Truth

From chapter four, you remember when the oldest living apostle John wrote to his friend Gaius in III John. John had walked with Jesus since he was a young man. For months he followed Him in the flesh and was invited to the Lord's most intimate experiences. He saw Jesus transformed on the mount with Moses and Elijah. He laid his head on the Lord's bosom during the Last Supper, and he went with the Lord into the Garden of Gethsemane. I'm sure you would agree this old apostle knew the Lord and His ways on a very special level. In this letter to his friend, John starts by sharing a prayer that he prayed above every other:

Beloved I pray that you may prosper in all things and be in health, just as your soul prospers (III John 2).

This introduction and prayer of John establishes several very important truths for the Christian. As I stated in the last chapter, we know that John would not pray something that was contrary to the will of God, and if he did, the Holy Spirit would not have recorded it and placed it in the canon of scripture. By inspiration of the Holy Spirit, John prays that they would prosper and that they would live in health. We need to realize it is God's will for His people to live in prosperity and health.

Someone once called me a health and wealth preacher (though I actually teach all the subjects of the New Testament). When I thought about that accusation, I realized that it is a lot better to preach health and wealth than sickness and poverty. By not understanding the words of the old apostle John and many such passages of scripture, the church world has preached a doctrine of sickness,

41

poverty, and defeat that has enabled the world to dominate the church, and kept many from entering the kingdom of God.

> ┌─ **RENEWING THE MIND KEY #13** ─┐
>
> GOD CREATED YOU TO PROSPER
> AND BE HEALTHY,
> NOT STRUGGLE THROUGH
> LIFE SICK AND POOR.

John goes on to explain how they will prosper, and live in health, when he says **...just as your soul prospers, III John 2.** All success in the Christian life starts on the inside of the person, and flows out. Jesus said in **Matthew 12:35, A good man out of the good treasure of his heart** (spirit and soul) **brings forth good things, and an evil man out of the evil treasure brings forth evil things.** When our soul prospers, we have a good treasure, which we can bring forth. When our soul is poor, or full of negative thoughts, attitudes and beliefs, we have an evil treasure so we can only bring forth defeat, despair and problems.

When we buy into the lie that the things outside of us are controlling the outcome of our lives, we enter into bondage. So many people really believe that if the government were different, or if their union would do something, or the company would make a new policy, that their life would be successful. The fact is those outer things may have some minor influence but what is in you is controlling the kind of life you experience. Outer circumstances may bring certain difficulties our way, but we choose how to deal with those things and whether to rise above them or be defeated by them. When you have prosperity and health on the inside, in your soul, you will bring it forth and see it manifested in every area of your life.

Third John 3-4 says, **For I rejoiced greatly when brethren came and testified of the truth that is in you, just as you walk in the truth. I have no greater joy than to hear that my children walk in truth.** The foundation of the prosperous soul is truth. The truth was in them and they walked in it. There is a twofold insight here that I believe is very important for us to see.

The first is that truth is God's Word. Jesus said in **John 8:31,32: . . . If you abide in My word, you are My disciples indeed. And you shall know the truth, and the truth shall make you free.** In **John 17:17** He said: **Sanctify them by Your truth. Your word is truth.** Only when we have heard, received, and renewed our minds to the Word of God, is the truth in us. This is the foundation for a prosperous soul. We must accept God's Word as the highest, and the final authority. It is higher than religious traditions, church decrees, family and cultural traditions, and every other order of life. God has exalted His Word even above His name. Heaven and earth will pass away, but the Word of God will stand forever.

Proverbs 4:20-23 says: **My son, give attention to my words; Incline your ear to my sayings. Do not let them depart from your eyes; Keep them in the midst of your heart; For they are life to those who find them, and health to all their flesh. Keep your heart with all diligence, for out of it spring the issues of life.** In this passage, we see the importance of God's Word as well as how the issues of life come out of the heart (spirit and soul), not from outer circumstances.

RENEWING THE MIND KEY #14

GOD'S WORD IS THE TRUTH,
WHICH IS THE BASIS
FOR ALL SUCCESS IN LIFE.

The second insight in III John, verse 4, is found in the definition of the Greek word we translate "truth." The Greek 'aletheia' literally means "nothing concealed." It is the reality at the basis of appearance. We could read this verse, "I have no greater joy than to hear that My children live with nothing concealed, walking in the reality of how they appear." This is a greatly needed revelation in our world today. Most people live lies of deception and hypocrisy.

It is normal and assumed that we will be phoney, say what others want to hear and do whatever it takes to get what we want. The truth is meaningless as we break our marriage vows, leave our children, lie to the IRS, and steal from our employer. The Christian is called to have a prosperous soul, one that is filled with truth and walks in truth; a life that is open and honest before all men.

The hypocrite is not one who denies the Lord, doesn't go to church and could not care less about godly living. The hypocrite is the one who is in church now and then, says "amen" to the preacher and acts like he loves the Lord. That is, until he gets to the car, where he cusses his wife, puts down the kids, and goes home to have a beer and watch the game. He's on the deacon board, but seldom pays his whole tithes, or follows through on his pledges. He acts nice to the people he works with, but gossips about them behind their backs.

The Greek word for hypocrite originally did not have a negative connotation. It described the actors in a stage play who used different masks to play various characters. The hypocrite was one who acted various roles in a play. New Testament writers began to use the word to describe the phoney or the person who hides and conceals the truth. Jesus called the religious leaders of His day "hypocrites" because they faked their dedication to God's Word and rather lived their man-made traditions (much like many Christians today). The prosperous soul is open and honest.

There is nothing concealed, and the face value is the real value.

If we have truth in us, and are walking in truth, there is a commitment and a passion in our lifestyle. Many Christians have a half-hearted commitment to truth; therefore, they have a half-hearted walk and relationship with the Lord. They believe the Bible, but there are parts they don't want to deal with. Many say they believe the Bible, but they don't want to pray with the Spirit, or lift up hands in worship, or bind an evil spirit, or give ten percent of their income to their church. Many hide things from their wife or husband, keeping feelings, hurts or things they've done concealed. They say they believe the truth, but they don't walk in it.

```
┌─  RENEWING THE MIND KEY #15  ─┐

    TO HAVE THE TRUTH IN US
    IS TO LIVE IT EVERY DAY.

└───────────────────────────────┘
```

Jesus said He wants us hot or cold, not lukewarm. The lukewarm person will be spewed out. I pray this is not seen as some kind of condemnation, but rather an opening of opportunity so you can have a prosperous soul and begin to prosper in all areas of your life. When the truth of God's Word, and an honest, open lifestyle, are in your soul, you are on your way to the blessing of God. Without God's Word, or with things concealed in your life, you can never experience the prosperous soul.

Every work that Satan is able to accomplish on earth is based on a lie. He is the father of all lies according to Jesus and when he gets someone to believe a lie, he can do his evil work in and through them. When society believes the lie that life is not sacred, then unborn babies, senior citizens, and anyone we don't want, can be legally murdered. When we believe that marriage is not a divine institution, than we can break our marriage vows, commit adultery, and sleep with whoever we want. Lies are the basis for every negative thing in our lives.

When you doubt God's Word, you believe Satan's word. God says He'll meet all our needs according to His riches in glory, but we often worry because we don't see how our needs will be met; so we believe a lie. God says He will heal all our diseases, but most Christians believe what a doctor says more than what God says (I don't mean we shouldn't go to doctors). The point is, we need to get real serious about truth. Through the Word of God, and an honest lifestyle, we can be the kind of people that the great apostle John rejoiced over. He had no greater joy than to see people have the truth in them and walk in the truth. This is why they had a prosperous soul, and how every part of their life prospered.

STEPS TO PERSONAL TRANSFORMATION

1. Do I believe God has created me to prosper and live
    in health?

2. What was the key to the prosperous soul in III John 2,3?

3. What areas of my life are hypocritical?

4. In what areas of my life do I know the truth but don't
    live it?

5. Is the truth of God's Word a valuable, foundational part
    of my life?

7

The Mind:
Control Center Of Your Life

The mind is an amazing, and powerful creation of God. No animal has a mind like yours;no machine, or computer can match its abilities; no human has tapped its full potential. It is the control center of our lives. It stores all experiences and learned material. It reasons, and creates information; it chooses from a myriad of options every day. It plans and sees into the future with an imagination that is unlimited. One has said ''a mind is a terrible thing to waste'' and yet we are wasting our minds daily. Even in the Christian world, we let our minds wander and lead us into mediocrity and negativity.

Romans 8:5,6 says:

For those who live according to the flesh set their MINDS on the things of the flesh, but those who live according to the Spirit, the things of the Spirit. For to be carnally MINDED is death, but to be spiritually MINDED is life and peace.

God established the mind as a center of reasoning, deciding, believing and envisioning. This passage in Romans 8:5,6 shows us that the mind decides whether we live in the flesh (which is the sin nature, negative desires, and the lower unregenerate part of man), or in the spirit (the godly, holy, recreated part of the Christian). If we set our minds on negative desires, imaginations, or experiences, we will eventually follow those thoughts, and begin to practice some degree of that negativity. **Proverbs 23:7: For as he thinks in his heart, so is he.**

It is well documented that what a child watches on TV affects his behavior. If it's a violent cartoon, he becomes agitated and aggressive. If it's Mr. Rogers, he has a more mild and stable demeanor. The man who watches pornographic movies will seek after the sexual fantasies he has watched. Much of the rape, incest, and sexual violence of our world can be traced to pornography. The things we set our mind on soon become behavior.

God designed our minds to be a great tool in learning His ways, and walking with Him for all our days on earth, as well as throughout eternity. We have the ability to grasp information and use it like no other creature. Like an iron trap, we create pictures and thoughts that stay with us our entire life. God's plan was that we would receive His Word and understand His ways, so we could fellowship with Him on His level forever.

Adam was to receive all the knowledge he needed from the Father, and not from evil or negative sources. The tree of the "knowledge (or thoughts) of good and evil" was there to give Adam a choice to learn from God or from the world. As long as he chose to receive God's Word, he prospered, and would have learned everything, and more than the tree of knowledge could ever give him. By taking the "knowledge" or "thoughts" of the world, Adam opened his mind, and his spirit to things contrary to God. The first effect was spiritual death, separation from God, and then, a way of living that eventually ended in physical death.

Through Jesus, we come back to God in our spiritual relationship when we are born again. But, our minds must be renewed to the knowledge of God, if we are to walk with Him on a daily basis. The goal of every Christian is to have the kind of relationship with the Lord that He originally planned in the beginning. Though we will never be back in the garden, with a born-again spirit and a renewed mind, we can walk with God again.

In Romans 8, Paul says, where you set your mind is the controlling factor between a spiritual life or a carnal life.

If we think on the things of the negative world around us, we will live carnal, negative, worldly lives. Paul says the carnal mind brings death. What kind of death? Spiritual death? If that is so, than most Christians have lost their salvation, and are spiritually dead, since most of us have unrenewed minds. No, the kind of death he is speaking of is separation from the blessing, and provision of God. The word *death* in the Bible literally means separation. To be *physically dead,* is to be separated from your body. To be *spiritually dead,* is do be separated from the eternal life of God.

The kind of death that the carnal mind brings is illustrated in Luke 15, in the parable of the prodigal son. You remember, he left the father, and wasted his inheritance on worldly living, and found himself eating the hogs' food. He was miserable, trying to make a living in a negative world. The scripture said, "When he came to his right mind" he went back to his father and repented of what he'd done. The father received him, blessed him, and threw a party because he was back. When the father saw him coming, he said, "My son was dead, but now is alive." The son was never physically dead, nor did he ever stop being his son. But, by leaving the father, and following his own carnal thoughts, he was separated or dead to the provision, and the protection of the father. He never received another inheritance, but at least he renewed his mind to come home.

RENEWING THE MIND KEY #16

WHERE YOU SET YOUR MIND
IS CONTROLLING WHERE YOU
GO IN LIFE.

Many Christians today are dead to the protection and provision of God. They live as though they were not children of the Father, with the same struggles and failures, as those who don't know God. Many Christians question their new birth because they go through the same challenges as the world and think they must really not be saved. There are those who have concluded the whole Christian faith is not real because of the negative things that have happened to them. They figure if God was real in their lives, those things would not have happened.

The problem is a lack of knowledge about the renewing of their minds. God is with them, and they really are His son or daughter, but they are living in the "hog pens" of life, because their mind is full of the thoughts of the world. This does not mean they seek after sin or evil, it may be worry, or fear, or unbelief, but their mind has opened the door for negativity, and they are separated from the protection and provision of the Father. The carnal mind is death (separation), but the spiritual mind is life and peace.

In the Williams New Testament, **Romans 8:5,6** says: **People who live by the standard set by their lower nature are usually thinking the things suggested by that nature.... To be thinking things suggested by the lower nature means death. For to be thinking things suggested by the spirit means life and peace.** The focus of our mind is the issue Paul is dealing with. When we focus on fleshly, sensual desires, or greedy materialistic desires or thoughts of anger, frustration, and violence, we are cut off from the life and peace of God, and find ourselves living out our thoughts. When we focus on the thoughts of God, the Word of God and the way God would have us live each day, then we have His provision and protection.

Isaiah 26:3 says: **You will keep him in perfect peace, whose mind is stayed on You, because he trusts in You.** "WHOSE MIND IS STAYED ON YOU" doesn't mean that we walk around thinking about nothing but God all the time. He knows we must do our job, look after the household. But **John 1:1** tells us **. . .the Word was God.** When we think in line with the Word of God, when our attitude is controlled by the Word of God, when we face life with the Word of God, then our mind is stayed on Him. That's when the life and peace of God are ours. People are looking for peace through drugs, romance, material things, religion, new-age philosophy, and many other things, but they never find it. It comes to those who have a spiritual mind by focusing their thoughts on the Word of God, and not allowing the thoughts of their flesh or the world to control them.

```
┌─ RENEWING THE MIND KEY #17 ─┐
  AS YOU REFOCUS YOUR MIND,
  YOU TAKE A NEW PICTURE
  OF YOUR FUTURE.
└─────────────────────────────┘
```

When I began to learn about the carnal, and the spiritual mind, I was a drug addict, and had almost destroyed my life. My thoughts were so crazy, that half the time I didn't know what I was thinking, and the other half I didn't want anyone else to know. To focus my mind on positive things was nearly impossible. If God had not said I could do it, I wouldn't have tried.

Through months of diligent work in learning the Word, and setting my mind on it, I began to get control of my thoughts, and build a spiritual mind. When I felt depressed, rather than having a drink or smoking a joint, I began to think on the destiny God planned for my life. When I was angry and wanted to punch someone's lights out, I began to think about the great love that motivated Jesus to give His life for me. When I started to worry about bills and money, I would stop and think about the promises of God to meet all my needs, and prosper my life. Soon I began to experience the peace of God, because my mind was stayed on Him. I began to see His provision, and blessing, because I was following the things of the Spirit, not the things of the flesh.

We must practice setting our minds on the things of God, not the things of the world. Meditation is simply thinking about something. We all meditate everyday, all day. The problem is, we often meditate on negative, selfish, fearful, worldly things. If we would think on, meditate on the Word of God day and night, **Psalm 1:3** says that you and I will be **like a tree planted by the rivers of water, that brings forth its fruit in its season, whose leaf also shall not wither; and whatever he does shall prosper.**

STEPS TO PERSONAL TRANSFORMATION

1. The control center of my life is the

   _____.

2. What things do I watch or think about that produce negative results in my life?

3. What areas of my mind are spiritual?

4. What areas of my mind are carnal?

5. What would I like to focus my thoughts on to build a new future?

8

Control Your Mind And Control Your Destiny

Second Corinthians 10:4,5: For the weapons of our warfare are not carnal but mighty in God for pulling down strongholds, casting down arguments and every high thing that exalts itself against the knowledge of God, bringing every thought into captivity to the obedience of Christ.

Paul is showing us through this passage where the greatest warfare of the Christian life really is. Though we do have to deal with demon spirits, Jesus has already defeated them, and given us His victory. However, we do not already have victory over the negative thoughts that can fill our minds, and control our life. Paul says there are "strongholds" that take root in the mind that must be brought down. *Stronghold* is a military term that describes a fortified place, or a place of domination, and control. Through the input of parents, secular schools, secular media, we all develop habits of thought that often contradict the Word of God. Some Christians have strongholds of fear and worry, others have strongholds of anger, or bitterness; there are strongholds of sexual sin, greed, selfishness, laziness....

```
┌─  RENEWING THE MIND KEY #18  ─┐

      WE CAN CAPTURE EVERY
       THOUGHT, AND BRING IT
          TO THE OBEDIENCE
       OF THE WORD OF GOD.

└───────────────────────────────┘
```

The first step in dealing with negative thoughts is to become aware, so we can "capture" these thoughts. To capture them, is to recognize them, and decide to reject them from your mind. Then we must make them submit to Christ, the Word of God. By rejecting the negative strongholds, and focusing on the thoughts of God, we pull down these strongholds and drive them out. Of course, this is not an instantaneous change. It takes discipline, and diligence, but it can be done. It is the way to control your life.

Paul says in **2 Timothy 1:7: For God has not given us a spirit of fear, but of power and of love and of a sound mind.** We can have a sound, disciplined, strong mind, a mind that thinks the thoughts of God, reasons according to the Word of God, and rejects the thoughts of the world. The lack of a sound, disciplined mind is a major problem in many people's lives today. The evidence is glaring as we realize the failure of public schools, find the number of hours the average person watches TV, and see the decline of real leaders, and the rise of welfare cases.

Most people do not exercise their minds. As one has said, "Most people are on mental birth control pills; they haven't given birth to a new thought in years." Lazy minds do not produce successful lives. Most of our nation's young people are better Nintendo players than readers. We'd rather watch someone on TV have an exciting life than to create one of our own. Many high school graduates don't have even the basics for success in life. We must get our minds in shape, before we let our world sink deeper in failure.

```
┌─ RENEWING THE MIND KEY #19 ─┐

    GOD ENABLES US TO HAVE A
    SOUND, DISCIPLINED MIND

└─────────────────────────────┘
```

Nothing, including the mind, gets better on its own. Everything left to itself is decaying, loosing power, and declining. You don't have to work to get out of shape. That will just happen. You have to work to get in, and stay in shape. You don't have to work to have a sloppy house. That comes naturally. You have to work to keep things clean and sharp. In the same way a lazy, negative mind comes naturally, but a sound, disciplined mind takes work. A mind left to itself will become stagnant, negative and sinful.

Mark 7:20-23 says: ...What comes out of a man, that defiles a man. For from within, out of the heart of men, proceed evil thoughts, adulteries, fornications, murders, thefts, covetousness, wickedness, deceit, licentiousness, an evil eye, blasphemy, pride, foolishness. All these evil things come from within and defile a man. We can't blame the devil when it's really *our* thoughts that open the door for evil and failure in our lives.

If we do not strive to develop a sound mind, these things that Jesus spoke of will begin to consume our minds. Society will not watch a movie, or listen to a song without sexual messages and evil overtones. Adultery is advised by many psychiatrists. Homosexuality is lauded, and fornication is expected, even of junior high kids. Horror movies, full of fear, hate, and murder, are some of the most popular. Rather than pull down the strongholds in our minds, and capture the thoughts that destroy us, we would rather change what is socially acceptable, make it "cool," or pass out condoms. **Mark 7:20** in *The Living Bible* says: **It is the THOUGHTLIFE that pollutes.**

The key to pulling down strongholds, capturing every thought, and developing a sound mind, is found in **Joshua 1:8: This Book of the Law shall not depart from your mouth, but you shall meditate in it day and night, that you may observe to do according to all that is written in it. For then you will make your way prosperous, and then you**

will have good success. Joshua was taking over leadership of the nation of Israel which was just preparing to possess its promised land. He had a very difficult position and God was giving him the key to his success or failure as a leader. Joshua was to keep God's Word in his mouth, and in his mind. If he did this, God promised him prosperity and good success. If his mouth was full of fearful and negative words, or if he filled his mind with worry and worldly thinking, he would fail and not possess the promises of God.

RENEWING THE MIND KEY #20

WE ALL MEDITATE EVERY DAY:
THE QUESTION IS, WHAT ARE WE
MEDITATING ON?

Though most people don't realize, we all meditate day and night. Meditation is simply thinking about something. The Hebrew word is to think on, ponder, mutter to oneself, or picture in the mind. It is impossible to not think about anything, so we meditate all our waking hours. The question is, what are you meditating on? Is your mind focused on the things of God, and His way of dealing with the issues you are facing? Or are you thinking on thoughts of anger, frustration, bitterness, anxiety, and so forth? God says the things you meditate on are deciding whether you prosper, and have good success, or struggle through life just trying to make a living.

Psalm 1:1-3 gives us more insight into controlling our thoughts, and the benefits of meditating on God's Word. **Blessed is the man who walks not in the counsel of the ungodly, nor stands in the path of sinners, nor sits in the seat of the scornful; But his delight is in the law of the Lord, and in His law he meditates day and night. He shall be like a tree planted by the rivers of water, that brings**

forth its fruit in its season, whose leaf also shall not wither; and whatever he does shall prosper. Once again, we see the importance of keeping our thoughts on the right things, and the positive outcome it will bring.

So many Christians think the reason they are poor and suffering, is because it is God's will for their life, when in fact, it is because of their negative mentality. They think on small, poverty-stricken, mediocre things, and that's what they have in life. If they would fill their thoughts with the Word of God, they would be like a fruitful tree that brings forth fruit, and their life would begin to prosper in every way. This does not mean money, although money is a part of it. It includes your marriage, family, relationships, church, career, and health. God wants every part of our lives to prosper, but the mind is the control center, so it must be programmed right.

Notice, David cautioned about who we walk through life with, and from where we receive counsel. Proverbs tells us that we become like the people we hang around. It is pretty obvious that you will not grow beyond the people that you spend the most time with. Look around at those closest to you. That is a picture of where you are or where you are going. If you like what you see, great; but if you don't want to live like those you hang around most, or if you want to continue to move forward in life, you'll have to get some new friends.

Mom and Dad may not be the best source to get counsel. Remember, their counsel will only take you as far as they have gone, no further. If they've never been there, they probably cannot help you get there. If we listen to the ungodly, the sinner, or the scornful, David says we will not be blessed. In other words, negative relationships will bring a curse. It is next to impossible to meditate on the things of God, and fellowship with worldly people. I'm not advocating that we hide from the world, but that we watch who we allow to influence our lives. We want to be an influence on people around us, so for that reason, we will have relationships with those who need the Lord. But, we must not allow them to pull us down to their level of negativity, and hinder our walk with God.

You may be in a situation with an unsaved spouse, or still living at home with unsaved parents. In these cases, you cannot leave the person, but you must guard your mind to keep your thoughts right, and not allow a negative environment to control you or drag you down.

┌ RENEWING THE MIND KEY #21 ┐

YOU MAY HAVE TO BUILD NEW
FRIENDSHIPS BEFORE YOU CAN
RENEW YOUR MIND TO
GOD'S WORD.

When a computer or a machine is programmed right, it gives the proper answer, data, or information and does the job it was created to do. When the mind is programmed right, in other words, it is renewed to the Word of God, and stays focused on it, then, our lives will prosper, and we will accomplish the things God created us to accomplish. You were not created to struggle through life and barely make it. God said you can take dominion, prosper, and have good success. As you control your mind, you control your life. Remember, you will prosper, and live in health, even as your soul prospers.

STEPS TO PERSONAL TRANSFORMATION

1. What three problems in my life may be strongholds in my mind?

2. What do I meditate on more than anything else?

3. How could I meditate on God's Word more?

4. Where do I receive most of my counsel from?

5. Which friends do I have that will help me renew my mind? Which friends may hinder me?

9

The Great Exchange

And do not be conformed to this world, but be TRANSFORMED BY THE RENEWING OF YOUR MIND, that you may prove what is that good and acceptable and perfect will of God, Romans 12:2.

Remember, to be transformed is to be changed in form, become completely different, go through a metamorphosis, to exchange one form for another. A caterpillar goes through a transformation that causes it to become something different than it was. It no longer crawls on branches and leaves; it now flies through the air. It no longer looks fuzzy and long; it now is a beautiful butterfly.

This is the kind of change that God wants in our lives. When we come to Him, it's not so we can join a religion or have something to do on Sunday mornings. We can become new species of beings, "new creations," as Paul said in **2 Corinthians 5:17: Therefore, if anyone is in Christ, he is a new creation; old things have passed away; behold, all things have become new.**

Of course, these are not physical changes, but spiritual, and mental as we renew our minds to the Word of God. This transformation causes us to be different than those in the world. We have a new way of thinking, a new way of acting, a new outlook on life, a new strength and power. We no longer go through the same troubles, and despair. When problems do come, we face them with the Word, and the Spirit of God, so we overcome, rather than being overcome.

RENEWING THE MIND KEY #22

WE CAN EXCHANGE OUR LACK FOR GOD'S ABUNDANCE.

The transformation, and change that God desires, starts in our spirit, when we are born again. The change, however, must continue in the soul/mental realm if we are going to accomplish all that God has for us. Notice in Romans 12:2, that the perfect will of God is only reached as we renew our minds.

Paul says in **Colossians 3:1-5,9,10:**

> **If then you were raised with Christ, seek those things which are above, where Christ is, sitting at the right hand of God.**

> **SET YOUR MIND ON THINGS ABOVE, NOT ON THINGS ON THE EARTH.**

> **For you died, and your life is hidden with Christ in God. When Christ who is our life appears, then you also will appear with Him in glory.**

> **Therefore put to death your members which are on the earth: fornication, uncleanness, passion, evil desire, and covetousness, which is idolatry.**

> **Do not lie to one another, since you have put off the old man with his deeds,**

> **AND HAVE PUT ON THE NEW MAN WHO IS RENEWED IN KNOWLEDGE ACCORDING TO THE IMAGE OF HIM WHO CREATED HIM.**

The great exchange is putting off the old man, and putting on the new man which is renewed in the knowledge of God. We give up the old way, and receive a whole new way of living. We leave the kingdom of the devil, and enter into the kingdom of God. We exchange our old way of thinking and acting for a new way. Paul says this new man is recreated according to the image of Christ. In **Romans 8:29** he says: **For whom He foreknew, He also predestined to be conformed to the image of His Son, that He might be the firstborn among many brethren.**

As we exchange our ways for His, we begin to experience this higher level of life that Paul is talking about. We are no longer controlled by the thoughts, attitudes, desires, and actions of the world, but we rise up to a new controlling source, the Spirit and Word of God. **Isaiah 55:7-9** says: **Let the wicked forsake his way, and the unrighteous man his THOUGHTS; let him return to the Lord, and He will have mercy on him; and to our God, for He will abundantly pardon. FOR MY THOUGHTS ARE NOT YOUR THOUGHTS, nor are your ways My ways, "says the Lord." For as the heavens are higher than the earth, so are My ways higher than your ways, and MY THOUGHTS THAN YOUR THOUGHTS.**

The Lord is telling us as we forsake our old thoughts and ways to exchange them for His, we will live a higher level of life. To have God's ways, we must have God's thoughts.

```
 ┌─ RENEWING THE MIND KEY #23 ─┐

      AS WE RENEW OUR MIND
    TO GOD'S HIGHER THOUGHTS,
     WE BEGIN TO EXPERIENCE
       GOD'S HIGHER WAYS.

 └─────────────────────────────┘
```

We've been seeing through verse after verse, that to have God's thoughts, we must renew our mind to His word. As we do so, we begin to rise up to His higher life. This is the great exchange. We give our low life, and get His high life. We give our death, and get His life. We give our sin, and get His righteousness. We give our sickness, and get His healing. We give our poverty, and get His prosperity. As we let go of what is ours in the natural realm of life, we receive what is His in the supernatural. Jesus said, **Whoever finds his [lower] life will lose [the higher life], and whoever loses his [lower] life on My account will find [the higher life], Matthew 10:39,** *The Amplified Bible.*

So many are afraid to let go of what is theirs to receive what is His. They know that what they have is not much, but it's all they've got, so they hang on to it. Though it is not giving them the life they want, they hang on to it. The alcoholic hates his booze but won't give it up. The poor person hates his poverty but won't change the things that keep him poor. The overweight person hates the fat but won't do what it takes to get fit. The lazy person hates the feeling of dissatisfaction with life but will not give up his TV and make something happen.

People hang on to the low life and give up the high life daily. Jesus said you have to get rid of the old wineskin, before you can receive the new wine. Though we all know it would be better, we can see others making changes and going for the higher life, but for some reason, we hang on to the low. We're tired of the old wine, but we're not ready to go for the new. There must be a point in life where you are not only tired of the old, but you are ready to do whatever it takes to have the new.

RENEWING THE MIND KEY #24

ONLY WHEN YOU LET GO
OF THE LOW LIFE, WILL
YOU FIND THE HIGH LIFE.

You must get to a place where you will make the exchange, whatever the cost. Sell out, burn your bridges, abandon your self, and go for it! At this point, you are in the process of proving the perfect will of God, and seeing the destiny that God has for you. It is risky, it is scary, it is a new territory, but it is the most exciting and rewarding step that you will ever take in life.

When I moved into the Drug Rehabilitation Center, and began to build a new life, I left every old friend, every old habit, and even my family (for a time) to start a new life for myself. I had to lose the lower life before I could find the high life. It certainly wasn't easy, but it was the greatest exchange I have ever made. Now I just continue to move with God, and keep the exchange going for the rest of my life. I've not arrived, I'll never be done, and I never want to quit.

STEPS TO PERSONAL TRANSFORMATION

1. How does transformation take place according to Romans 12:2?

2. Change starts in the _____ but must continue in the soul or _____ realm.

3. What specific thoughts of God have caused my life to rise up to a higher level?

4. What parts of the "old man" or "low life" have I hung on to that stopped growth and change?

5. How do I feel about the risk of exchanging what I have for what God has?

10

Five Areas
Where Our Minds
Must Be Renewed

The following points are areas of life, that we must have God's perspective on if we are to move forward in our Christian walk at all. These are areas where many people have little knowledge of the truth according to God's Word, and consequently, struggle through life far below the perfect will of God. I am not going to deal with these things in an in-depth way. My desire is to give you an introduction and stir your thoughts about them. Seek after greater knowledge and insight in these areas, because they are foundational to your success in the Lord and in life.

I.
WE MUST BELIEVE THAT GOD HAS A PLAN AND A DESTINY FOR OUR LIVES.

Most people in our world today live life to get by. They have no sense of purpose or destiny. To pay the monthly bills, get a new car or maybe a bigger house is about all the destiny they think about. In fact, the Bible teaches that before God made the earth, He knew you and planned a great life for you. The average Christian never fulfills the destiny of God because they know nothing about it, and they live for lower goals and desires.

Ephesians 1:3-6 says: **Blessed be the God and Father of our Lord Jesus Christ, who has blessed us with every spiritual blessing in the heavenly places in Christ, just as HE CHOSE US IN HIM BEFORE THE FOUNDATION OF**

THE WORLD, that we should be holy and without blame before Him in love, HAVING PREDESTINED US to adoption as sons by Jesus Christ to Himself, according to the good pleasure of His will.

Ephesians 1:11 tells us:....**BEING PREDESTINED according to the PURPOSE of Him who works all things according to the counsel of His will.** In **Ephesians 2:10,** *The Amplified Bible,* we read: **For we are God's handiwork, recreated in Christ Jesus, that we may do those good works which God predestined for us....** God's predestination, according to **Romans 8:29,** is always based on His foreknowledge. **For whom He foreknew, He also predestined to be conformed to the image of His Son, that He might be the firstborn among many brethren.** In other words, you are not a puppet on a string that has no choice in life. In fact, God gave you a will, and then before the foundation of the world, looked out through history, and saw the choices you would make. Based on the foreknowledge of your choices, He planned a fulfilling, rewarding, satisfying life for you.

Our greatest mission in life is not to establish our own dreams, and work until they come to pass. Our mission is to seek God, find His plan and purpose for our lives, and then go for it with all that is within us. Most people in this world are unhappy, going to work everyday, because they do not feel they are fulfilling any purpose or destiny. Many try to do things they were not called to do, merely emulating or trying to be like someone else. Whether you are to teach, raise children, pastor a church, build airplanes or houses, God has a great plan for your life that will offer the maximum fulfillment you can experience on earth.

Here are eight steps to discovering your destiny in the Lord:

1)   Know the real desire of your heart, not what someone else wants you to do or the fleeting fantasies of your mind (Psalm 37:3,4),

2) Know what stirs your passion, drive and zeal (John 2:17),

3) Know what flows naturally with your gifts and talents (Romans 12:4-6),

4) Seek counsel from mature Christian friends and leaders (Proverbs 11:14,18:1),

5) Listen to the witness of the Holy Spirit in your spirit (Romans 8:14-16),

6) Know what you can give yourself totally, 100% to (1 John 3:16),

7) Know what produces good results or fruit (Matthew 12:33),

8) Follow the peace of God inside you (Colossians 3:15).

II.
WE MUST BELIEVE THAT OUTSIDE CIRCUMSTANCES DO NOT CONTROL OUR LIVES; IT IS WHAT IS ON THE INSIDE OF US THAT DECIDES HOW WE LIVE AND WHAT WE ACCOMPLISH.

It's easy to blame the government, society, family, or events for the way we are today. Most people will agree with you when you begin to complain about the things around you that you think are controlling your life. Whether it's the traffic that made you mad, the government that took your money, the boss that did you wrong, or the spouse that keeps you upset. In reality, you are making choices about all these things. Your involvement with them, and how you deal with them is determined by you. While there are accidents, and situations that we don't choose or want, the fact is, we decide how to deal with them.

When my close friends lost a two-month-old baby to Sudden Infant Death Syndrome, they had to decide how to deal with it. It devastated their lives (and mine) for a time, but then they rose up with faith, and love, and went on to minister to others, and live their destiny in God. The negative thing could not control them and throw them into a life of bitterness, anger or doubt. It is easy to let the negatives of life become the controlling factors, but we don't have to. We can rise up, take control of our thoughts and feelings, and go on with life.

Jesus said in **Matthew 12:35: A good man out of the good treasure of his heart brings forth good things, and an evil man out of the evil treasure brings forth evil things.** It's not what is around you that controls your future, it's what's in you. In fact, your future is in your heart.

III.
WE MUST BELIEVE THAT GOD DESIRES FOR US TO HAVE AN ABUNDANT LIFE IN EVERY REALM; IF WE GIVE THE BEST, WE WILL HAVE THE BEST.

Regardless of the economy, or marketplace, God is a God of abundance. He told Abraham, ''I am El Shaddai,'' the God that is more than enough. Abraham became a very rich man as he walked with God (Genesis 12-17). His riches were not only in finances but in family, relationships, and spirituality. Isaac, his son, prospered in a land of famine and recession as he walked with God and obeyed His Word.

Jesus said in **John 10:10: . . . I have come that they may have life, and that they may have it more abundantly.** In **Luke 6:38** we're told: **Give, and it will be given to you: good measure, pressed down, shaken together, and running over will be put into your bosom. For with the same measure that you use, it will be measured back to you.** The prophet Malachi tells us to bring our tithes (one tenth) into the church, that there will be food in God's house, and that the Lord can open the windows of heaven and pour you out a blessing. God wants you to enjoy His creation, all the good things He has put on the earth. Nice things are not here for Satan's people to enjoy their sin more. The best properties were not created for taverns or casinos; they are for the people of God to do the work of God and enjoy their relationship with Him. God did not put Adam and Eve in a desert; He put them in a beautiful garden because He wanted them to be blessed.

As we renew our minds to the Word of God, and live according to His principles, we will see His abundance spiritually, mentally, physically and financially. We do not live for the blessings, but as we live for God, His abundant life, and His blessings are ours.

IV.
WE MUST ORDER OUR LIFE IN A BALANCED WAY, AND KEEP OUR PRIORITIES IN LINE WITH GOD'S WILL.

If your job takes priority over your family, you will soon lose them, as many in our nation have already found. Over half our marriages are failing, and the main reason is wrong priorities in one or both spouses. When you put the wrong things first in life, you fail. There is no way around the reality of right priorities. One of our nation's top business speakers and consultants teaches that you cannot take time for your family, and do all that is necessary to get ahead in business. Many buy into that philosophy, and sacrifice their family, health, and peace of mind.

It may be true that without the Lord, you cannot prosper without giving everything else up. With God, however, you can! If you will make Jesus the top priority of your life, then He will enable you to succeed in business, family, as well as other areas of your life. Jesus said, **But seek first the kingdom of God and His righteousness, and all these things shall be added to you, Matthew 6:33.**

Here's a simple way to examine your schedule and priorities:

FAITH: Relationship with the Lord through regular prayer, Bible study, and church attendance.

FITNESS: Mental/Physical health through renewing the mind, study, regular exercise, proper rest and proper diet.

FAMILY: Strong, happy relationships with spouse and children through daily communication and time together.

FELLOWSHIP: Healthy relationships with friends that build you up and help you toward your goals in life.

FINANCE: A fulfilling career, that brings prosperity and enough to fulfill your dreams.

FUN: Recreation and activities, that enable you to enjoy the blessings you have received.

V.
WE MUST BE EXCELLENT!!
EXCELLENCE IS A KEY TO EXPERIENCING GOD'S WILL IN EVERY REALM OF LIFE.

We live in a world where just getting by is viewed as good. We must realize that according to God's perspective, "good" is the enemy of "best." On the job, many people don't do their best; they do enough to get by. They reason there is no use to doing the best job they can because they get paid the same, no matter what they do. The problem is, they don't realize there is more to their pay than the check they receive. New opportunities from the Lord, increases, and prosperity come to those who are faithful over little. If you give your best, when nobody but God is looking, you will soon be "ruler over much" (Luke 16:10-12).

Daniel was a prophet in the Old Testament, who was taken captive into Babylon as a young boy. His family was killed, and his nation destroyed. He was a refugee in a great city with no family or people to help him. Babylon was a new age, secular humanist, demonic place, that did not serve God in any way. In spite of all the things against him, Daniel rose up to be a leader in that nation, and influenced many people.

Daniel 5:12: Inasmuch as an excellent spirit, knowledge, understanding, interpreting dreams, solving riddles, and explaining enigmas were found in this Daniel, whom the king named Belteshazzar, now let Daniel be called, and he will give the interpretation. Because of his "excellent spirit," he was called upon and respected by the leaders of Babylon. If we as Christians would get rid of the "barely get by" attitude and begin to go for excellence in every area of life, we, too, would have influence on our nation.

Mediocrity is a curse that causes people, families, businesses, and ministries, to exist far below their potential. Only through excellence do we reach the top of our abilities. Because mediocrity is normal, and so much easier to attain, we must "fight " for excellence. It must be a drive and a passion that gets us up earlier, causes us to stay longer, and motivates us to give more than is required.

Psalm 8:1 says: **O Lord, our Lord, how EXCELLENT IS YOUR NAME in all the earth, you who set Your glory above the heavens!** God's name describes His nature, His character, His being. When He says His name is excellent, He is telling that His character, nature, being, and everything about Him are excellent. God is not involved with mediocrity, and lukewarmness. He goes for the best every time and is always excellent.

We must start where we are, and use whatever we have, but the point is, don't settle for less than excellent. You may not be there now (I know I'm not), but you're on the way. Don't accept a mediocre life. Fight for excellence in everything.

Be excellent in your work.

Be excellent in your parenting.

Be excellent in your relationships and communication.

Be excellent in your home.

Be excellent in your dress.

BE AN EXCELLENT PERSON!

STEPS TO PERSONAL TRANSFORMATION

1. Do I believe God has a plan for my life?

2. What parts of God's plan am I aware of at this point in my life?

3. What outside circumstances do I allow to control my life?

4. Am I willing to give the best that I might receive the best?

5. What priorities in my life are out of balance?

11
Change: Learn To Love It

Change and growth must become something we love, not just endure. If it is always a struggle to face truth, and confrontation, we will look for ways to avoid it. When we fall in love with the truth and the results that it produces in our lives, we will seek for it and always move forward in the Lord. It's like the runner who finds that place of ecstasy as he runs. At first it is a labor and a discipline, but then comes a place where he feels like he's floating. He's beyond having to force each step. Now his legs are moving seemingly effortlessly, and he enjoys the miles that drift by. While change and growth will never be effortless (neither is exercise), there is a place where it is not a forced discipline and struggle.

Proverbs 9:7-9 shows us the person who despises change, and the person who loves it: **He who reproves a scoffer gets shame for himself, and he who rebukes a wicked man gets himself a blemish. Do not reprove a scoffer, lest he hate you; REBUKE A WISE MAN, AND HE WILL LOVE YOU. Give instruction to a wise man, and he will be still wiser; TEACH A JUST MAN, AND HE WILL INCREASE IN LEARNING.**

Those who are scoffers, who have a rebellious, stagnant spirit, will always react, when confronted with truth. They don't want to change, or don't have the self-esteem to look at their faults, so they hate the one who told them the truth. You can examine yourself in this area by asking yourself, ''Do I love the people that challenge me to change, or do I dislike and avoid them?''

```
┌─ RENEWING THE MIND KEY #25 ─┐
│  TO MAKE GROWTH AND CHANGE  │
│     A PART OF YOUR LIFESTYLE,│
│       YOU MUST LOVE IT.     │
└─────────────────────────────┘
```

Most people build a circle of friends that help them stay where they are in life and not make changes. They endorse each other's complacency, and encourage each other to stay the same. If one person tries to break out of the rut, the others pressure them not to move on, lest they be left behind. There is a kind of group pressure that stops growth. To renew the mind and go on in life, you must leave friends like these and develop new relationships. A real friend will not slow you down but help you to grow and go on in life. Anyone who is not helping you fulfill your destiny is hurting you. Proverbs says if you are wise, you will love the one who rebukes you. If you are a fool, you will hate them.

Sometimes the people closest to us, like parents, can be the most detrimental to our future. They subconsciously want to hold you where they are, and keep you from growing. Without realizing it, they feel challenged if you move on so they try to stop you. **Proverbs 13:20** says, **He who walks with wise men will be wise, but the companion of fools will be destroyed.** Check out who you are walking with, who you spend the most time with. They may be the next change you need to make.

Proverbs 12:1: Whoever loves instruction loves knowledge, but HE WHO HATES REPROOF IS STUPID. We must decide to love the process of change, though it may not feel good at the time. If we avoid it, and despise it, we will become fools and stupid. It's kind of like exercise; it may not feel enjoyable while you're sweating, but when your clothes fit good, and your waist is not hanging over your belt, you are glad you went through the pain.

Our society exalts the rebel and the independent person. While there are positive aspects to being unique and a non-conformist, God says ...**rebellion is as the sin of witchcraft, and stubbornness is as iniquity and idolatry...,1 Samuel 15:23.** When we resist change and growth, we actually open ourselves to an evil spirit and bring all kinds of negativity into our lives. Christians who have refused to flow with the Spirit of God and have settled into a religious rut, have become some of the most rebellious, bigoted and stubborn people ever. The greatest hate and prejudice have always come from religious people.

RENEWING THE MIND KEY #26

THE BIGGEST CHANGE YOU MAY
HAVE TO MAKE IS WHO YOU
SPEND YOUR TIME WITH.

The wise in heart will receive commands, but a prating fool will fall, Proverbs 10:8. The way of a fool is right in his own eyes, but he who heeds counsel is wise, Proverbs 12:15. We all want to be right, but the fact is, we are never right all the time. Rather than seeking to be corrected when we are wrong, human nature hides, denies and defends itself. I know many people who would rather fail at whatever they are doing, than admit they had made a mistake. Only a fool thinks he's always right; the wise man seeks counsel.

The following is a list of Proverbs that teach us to love change and correction. If we follow the wisdom of God, we will prosper. If we refuse to listen and grow, we will fail.

Proverbs 6:23

For the commandment is a lamp, and the law is light; reproofs of instruction are the way of life.

Proverbs 9:7-9

He who reproves a scoffer gets shame for himself, and he who rebukes a wicked man gets himself a blemish. Do not reprove a scoffer, lest he hate you; rebuke a wise man, and he will love you. Give instruction to a wise man, and he will be still wiser; Teach a just man, and he will increase in learning.

Proverbs 11:14

Where there is no counsel, the people fall; But in the multitude of counselors there is safety.

Proverbs 13:1

A wise son heeds his father's instruction, but a scoffer does not listen to rebuke.

Proverbs 13:18,20

Poverty and shame will come to him who disdains correction, but he who regards reproof will be honored. He who walks with wise men will be wise, but the companion of fools will be destroyed.

Proverbs 15:10,12,22

Harsh correction is for him who forsakes the way, and he who hates reproof will die. A scoffer does not love one who reproves him, nor will he go to the wise. Without counsel, plans go awry, but in the multitude of counselors they are established.

Proverbs 15:31-33

The ear that hears the reproof of life will abide among the wise. He who disdains instruction despises his own soul, but he who heeds reproof gets understanding. The fear of the Lord is the instruction of wisdom, and before honor is humility.

STEPS TO PERSONAL TRANSFORMATION

1. What must I change in order to love the process of change?

2. Do any of my friends bring pressure that hinders me from changing?

3. What does Proverbs 9:7-9 tell me about receiving instruction?

4. How do I apply Proverbs 11:14 to the decisions I make?

5. Do I love the one that corrects me?

12
No Quick Fixes!

If you've made it this far in this message, you must have a real desire for change in your life. This is obviously not the most thrilling, exciting, spine-tingling message that can be studied. I have often wished (momentarily) that the Lord would have allowed me to emphasize healing, or prosperity, or miracles, or the Holy Spirit in our ministry. But no, I'm called to teach *Renewing The Mind*. Certainly not a spontaneous, miraculous kind of teaching.

In today's world, we like the quick and the easy. If God would supernaturally remove all problems, attitudes, and sin, we would all line up to "get it together" by the power of God. Most people are looking for that quick fix that will make their life better. Whether it's finances, or weight loss, building relationships, or breaking bad habits, if there is a pill, a program, or an easy way, we'll go for it.

We live in a "micro-wave" world. We want it quick and easy.

* "Let's not wait for a solid relationship to grow; let's have sex *now*!"

* "Why get married? We'll just live together."

* "Solving problems is too hard; let's just get divorced!"

* "Proper diet and exercise takes too long! I need a pill."

* "Saving money is hard work. I need another credit card."

* "Children are too much responsibility. I'm having an abortion."

I could go on and on with the thoughts that prevail in our world concerning taking the easy way. The sad truth is that this same attitude prevails in the church. As I said, if God would do a miracle, every Christian would line up for change. But if it takes discipline, effort, and renewing of the mind, then forget it! Most Christians do not grow spiritually after their first year or so in the Lord. It's not that they don't love God or that they don't want to go on with God. It's that they were raised to think learning, growing, and changing stop when you get out of high school or college. Then, they spend the rest of their lives defending what they know, rather than seeking to grow.

```
┌─ RENEWING THE MIND KEY #27 ─┐

  MOST PEOPLE SPEND THEIR
  ADULT YEARS DEFENDING
  WHAT THEY KNOW, RATHER
  THAN SEEKING TO GROW.

└─────────────────────────────┘
```

We have not accepted the fact that our grandparents had some truth that we have let slip away. The previous generation knew that good things take time. A well-cooked meal, a well-built house or a loving relationship cannot be made in a micro-wave. Life was slower for them, and so quality and endurance was more common. It wasn't so important to get it all as quick and easy as possible. The good things were worth the wait and the work to get them. I hope this isn't coming across as some "remember the good-ol'-days message," but we really have lost some values that our grandparents had.

Until 1945, the United States had no national debt, and taxes were at a minimum (if any). Then we slipped into the age of fast factory-built merchandise, fast marriage and divorce, fast financial profits and losses, fast credit and fast foods. While some of these things are fine, the overall effect on the nation is devastating. We may never pay off the national debt and the average person leaves an inheritance of lack and shortage, instead of abundance to their children. Over half of our marriages fail. We kill thousands of children daily, and sexually-transmitted diseases touch nearly every family in some way. The get-it-quick and easy life has only brought pain, poverty and despair to our world.

In the church, this is translated into an attitude of lukewarmness and mediocrity. Many churches condone the worldly lifestyles of their members, rather than teaching them to live in holiness. Some leaders give them the philosophy it takes, but don't challenge them to change and grow. Much of the Body of Christ has sacrificed teaching and preaching of the Word of God for religion, and social shows that attract the masses.

It's one thing to have a crowd but entirely a different thing to have a church. There are many church attenders, but few real members. **Psalm 92:13** says: **Those who are planted in the house of the Lord shall flourish.** The solid, long-term, committed Christian is the one who sees the real blessings of the Lord. The quick and easy Christian never does. To have all that God has for you, you must follow His plan daily. Growth doesn't come with the laying on of hands from the pastor, or the miraculous moving of the Spirit. Growth comes from renewing the mind to the Word of God and practicing the living of that Word every day. Renewing the mind is not the most thrilling message in the Bible (and certainly not the only message we should study), but it is the master key to all Christian growth.

As we give ourselves to continued change and growth, we develop a flow in life that keeps us free from the negativity of stagnation, and keeps us moving in the will of God. Jesus said we must "continue" in His Word, before we would know the truth. Then the truth would set us free. Those who don't continue will never see freedom.

STEPS TO PERSONAL TRANSFORMATION

1. What things have I done in the "quick and easy" way that did not produce good results?

2. What things do I defend that may be hindering my life?

3. Am I planted in a local church?

4. Am I involved with the Word of God or just religious activities?

5. Do I value the truth of God's Word and continue in it?

13

The Master Key

At the beginning of this book, I said its purpose was to assist you in becoming all that is possible in the Lord. It really is my prayer that you fulfill your potential in every aspect of life. This must become your goal as well. The reason that many drift and stagnate in life, is because they never decide to go farther. They sit by the side of the road, but never look down the road and go for it.

Where there is no revelation, people cast off restraint, Proverbs 29:18, or as the *King James Version* states: **Where there is no vision, the people perish.** Without a goal and a purpose, we perish. The suicidal person is one with no hope, no vision of a future, no reason to go on in life any farther. Our vision is the reason we get out of bed, the reason we read books like this one, the reason we go on. It may be a vision of raising the kids, building a company, starting a ministry or buying a house. That vision will give you a certain amount of impetus to grow and change.

It seems most people get caught at some point in life with a "maintenance vision." They have the house, the kids are raised, and the business is operating. Rather than seeking the Lord to see what He has in mind for them at this point in their life they begin to maintain. Thinking they will enjoy life for a while they kick back into maintenance mode. The problem is that you cannot *maintain* in life. If you are not moving forward, you are moving backward. It's like swimming upstream; you either keep swimming or start floating downstream. Soon these folks feel unwanted, or unimportant, and they get depressed, not realizing why. Where there is no vision, the people perish.

Many people die in their second year of retirement because of a lack of vision. The physical problems that may arise are merely symptoms of their stagnation in life. Many die shortly after the death of a spouse because their vision for life was as a team. When part of the team dies, the vision is over. God wants us to stay young and live long. That means we must keep a vibrant vision of growth and change all our life. We must make it the passion of our life to be all we can be in God, go as far as we can go with God, and fulfill all that we can fulfill of the will of God. Paul said he "finished his course" and was ready to go on and be with the Lord. You can finish your course too.

RENEWING THE MIND KEY #28

THERE'S MORE TO YOUR
LIFE THAN
"MAKING A LIVING."

"Making a living" is not a motivating vision it is a *maintenance* vision that will soon have you floating down the river. So many live to get the bills paid, take a vacation or buy "more stuff." There is more to life then that vision. When you've accomplished these things, there is an empty feeling of, "Is that all there is?" If you have a burning passion of God's will for your life every day, you will have that spark of life.

Gideon was a young man with no vision. He saw himself as weak, poor, and unable to do anything about his circumstances. One day the angel of the Lord came to him while he was hiding in a winepress, threshing out wheat to make some bread. He was afraid that the Midianites would find him and take away what little wheat he had for his family. This was not a man who was making plans for his future. Gideon was just trying to make a living.

The angel of the Lord said to Gideon in **Judges 6:12: The Lord is with you, you mighty man of valor!** These words were totally contrary to Gideon's mind-set, his feelings, and his lifestyle. He had never been mighty as a champion, a warrior, or a leader. He had never been a man of valor, honor, esteem or influence. He was a scared little guy, trying to get through life. But God said, "You are a mighty man of valor!" In the next few chapters of the book of Judges, we see the Lord take Gideon through a series of events that helped him renew his mind to God's Word, and purpose for his life.

Gideon argued with God that he was not a mighty man but a loser, and a failure, but the Lord would not allow him to hang on to his mediocre lifestyle. Finally, Gideon began to accept what God said about him and reject what he had believed for so long. There were three areas that God led Gideon to change before he could fulfill his destiny:

1)   His self-esteem,

2)   His vision for life, and

3)   His relationships with people.

Gideon had to renew how he thought about himself, how he thought about his future and who he was involved with. With these changes made, he went on to defeat his enemy, the Midianites, deliver his nation from bondage, and be one of the greatest judges of Israel.

Gideon had the potential for greatness in him all the time. It wasn't that God made him something he had not been before. Everything that he needed was on the inside of him. God simply led him to renew the things that were holding him back and go on to fulfill his destiny.

```
┌─ RENEWING THE MIND KEY #29 ─┐

      YOU ARE A MIGHTY
    MAN/WOMAN OF VALOR;
     IT'S TIME YOU FOUND
       THE REAL YOU!!
└─────────────────────────────┘
```

I pray the truths you have read will enable you to make the necessary changes to go on and fulfill your destiny. You have what it takes to prosper and live in health. You have inside of you the potential to make a difference in your family, city and nation.

GO FOR IT! Take the risk! Discover the destiny God has had in mind for you all along. Remember, you will prove God's perfect will only as you are "TRANSFORMED BY THE RENEWING OF YOUR MIND."

STEPS TO PERSONAL TRANSFORMATION

1. Do I feel motivated to fulfill my full potential?

2. What is my vision for the future?

3. In what aspects of life am I merely maintaining?

4. How could I relate my situation in life to Gideon's?

5. Have I decided to be the mighty man/woman of valor that God has called me to be?

Other Books By Casey Treat

Living the New Life

God's Word for Every Circumstance

Setting Your Course

Reaching Your Destiny

Church Management

Being Spiritually Minded

Blueprint for Life

Fighting for Excellence In Leadership

Building Leaders That Build A Church

Errors of the Prosperity Gospel

Available from your local bookstore
or by writing:

Harrison House

P. O. Box 35035 • Tulsa, OK 74153

To contact the author, write or call:

Casey Treat Ministries • Christian Faith Center
P. O. Box 98800 • Seattle, WA 98198

(206) 824-8188